# THE ADVENTURES OF VINCE THE CAT

CW00540593

## VINCE GOES TO PARIS

**1st Edition**

with love Heidi

By Heidi Bryant

# PUBLISHING DETAILS

Published in 2018 by Ipsum Agency
(www.ipsum-agency.com)

Some of the proceeds of this book will be donated to Plan International UK (Registered Charity).

**W**   catnapstories.com
**f**   facebook.com/catnapstories
⊙   @catnapstories

# DEDICATION

This book is dedicated to my wonderful mum
Jackie – who has supported me wholeheartedly
throughout my life and without whom this book
wouldn't have existed.

Thank you for believing in me.

# THANK YOU

* Mum and Dad for everything you do to help me
* Jonathan, Anna, Robin, Karen, Christelle, Reinet, Tiffany, Giuseppe, Chris, Mark, for your support and your belief in me
* Maman Walsh for inspiring my love of languages
* Prayan Animation Studio for the beautiful illustrations (prayananimations.com)
* Nigel and Nick for your support with the print (maximprint.co.uk)
* Lucy and Jen (printondemand-worldwide.com)
* Amanda for bringing my ideas to life
* Jaime for the amazing Cat font (jaimevicente.com)

# VINCE GOES TO PARIS

**W**hile children were outside hunting for Easter eggs on a bright Easter Sunday morning, something magical was going on in the cupboard under the stairs at grandma's house.

Misty, a lovely calm and purry tortoiseshell cat was having her kittens. The last of four kittens to be born that day was a very special little grey and white kitten.

Misty and her kittens were nestled into a box which Grandma had lined with an old curtain, she licked Vince and the other kittens, purring while she did.

Grandma had a granddaughter called Heidi and the little girl had been waiting for this very special day for what seemed a lifetime.

Heidi didn't have any brothers or sisters of her own and was so looking forward to meeting the new kittens.

She knew that she was going to love the new kittens and she was hoping that her mummy would let her have one to keep for herself. It would be very exciting to see them. Maybe she would know right away which one she wanted.

**C**arrying an Easter egg that
she had found as a present for grandma she
ran up the path to grandma's house and shouted.

"Grandma! It's me!"

Grandma hurried out of the kitchen holding her
finger in front of her lips.

"Shh Heidi," she said quietly as she beckoned
the little girl forward and opened the door to the
cupboard under the stairs.

"Oh grandma, have they? Are they?" Heidi
whispered.

**H**astily giving the Easter egg to her grandma Heidi dropped to her knees in front of the little box.

Misty looked up at her and purred loudly. She was very proud of her new kittens.

Snuggled next to the little grey and white kitten was a sister who was tortoiseshell just like her mother, a brother who was black with white paws and a white bib, and another sandy coloured brother.

**H**eidi was surprised to see so many different coloured kittens – they were all pretty but she had never seen a grey and white kitten before and she reached forward and stroked the tiny little grey and white head with her finger.

Could this be the little kitten that she was going to have one day to take home? Heidi looked down at the little grey and white body and felt such love for the little creature, yes, this was going to be her kitten.

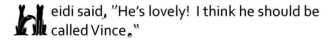 eidi said, "He's lovely! I think he should be called Vince."

"Well that is a funny name for a kitten, but I think he may well be your very own kitten so you should be the one to choose his name." Grandma said.

"Really grandma?" Heidi said "Really? Oh thank you grandma, thank you so much!"

In the days after they were born, the kittens could hear voices and they could feel the warmth from their mother, and they were happy snuggled up and drinking her warm milk.

She would wash them with her raspy tongue and that felt very good but they could not see her yet.

Heidi visited them every day after school and watched as, little by little, the kittens began to grow. She would stroke all of them but she always gave special attention to Vince, and she was sure that he knew the touch of her finger on his little head.

She picked him up and looked at his tiny ears and his little nose, his tiny paws and his fur that was so soft and finally his little tail. It was small now but Heidi knew that it would grow big and fluffy.

The Adventures of Vince The Cat – Vince Goes to Paris

**M**ostly Heidi just thought how perfect he was. His brothers and sisters were beautiful too but there was something about little Vince that Heidi just knew meant that they would be together for life.

She would look after him when he was small and then when he got bigger maybe they could go out together.

Oh the adventures they would have!

When she went to bed at night Heidi would imagine all the things that she would do with Vince when he was big enough.

She could hardly wait!

Everyday she would notice small changes that meant that the kittens were getting bigger, and she laughed at their round little tummies, full up with the warm milk from their mother.

Heidi desperately wanted to take the new kitten home, this was a kitten who could be her lifelong friend.

Then one day, when Heidi arrived, Vince had opened his eyes for the first time, and he looked right at her! He could now see his mum and his three siblings.

"Can I take Vince home yet grandma?"

"Not yet Heidi and besides which you haven't asked mummy yet, have you?"

"Oh, no." Heidi said. "I hope she says yes, she has to say yes!"

As she hurried home to ask mummy if she could have Vince Heidi kept saying, "please say yes, please say yes, please say yes."

What if mummy said no?

Heidi could not imagine what she would do then. She and Vince were meant to be friends for life, she knew that, but would mummy understand that too? Maybe if Heidi promised to do lots of chores in the house? Maybe if she promised to keep her room clean, always? Maybe if she promised to do her homework without mummy nagging?

The Adventures of Vince The Cat – Vince Goes

*"Oh* please say yes!" she said out loud as she hurried up the garden path. When she got home, Heidi sat down at the kitchen table to drink a glass of milk.

"How are the new kittens, Heidi?" Her mummy asked.

"They are growing up and today their eyes are open! Vince looked right at me!" Heidi said.

"Mum, when the kittens are old enough could I have Vince? Grandma says it will be alright." Heidi held her breath.

"Well Heidi having a cat is a big responsibility, you will have to feed him and look after him. Do you think you could do that? And I don't mean just for a little while, I mean, for as long as he lives. That will be very many years."

"Oh yes mummy, I know I could, I love Vince already and I will always look after him."

"Well alright then, Heidi, when he is big enough you can bring him home."

"Oh mummy, you're the best!" Heidi ran to hug her mummy.

Grandpa had made a playpen out in the garden for the kittens to play in and when Heidi came over he would lift her into the playpen with the four kittens, where they would play together for hours.

They tried to run on their little legs, they sometimes fell over each other and chased little toys on strings that Heidi held up for them.

She loved the little meowing sounds they made and soon she could recognise Vince's voice over the others. When the kittens were tired Vince would always come over to Heidi and sleep on her lap while the other three kittens curled up together.

The Adventures of Vince The Cat – Vince Goes to Paris

The Adventures of Vince The Cat – Vince Goes to Paris

**V**ince was getting bigger now and Heidi needed to use her whole hand to stroke him. Heidi loved him and there was no doubt that he loved her back.

When Vince was old enough and no longer needed his mum, it was finally time for him to go to live with Heidi in her house. Heidi had made lots of toys for him and with mummy had made a lovely bed for him to take naps in. They had bought him special kitten food too.

Everyone in the house loved Vince and he purred happily when they stroked him, but it was Heidi he loved and wherever she went he was right behind her. When she was asleep he would be in his little bed beside hers although sometimes he would creep in beside her, his little body vibrating as he purred loudly and rubbed his face on hers.

Heidi would look into his eyes and smile at him, and Vince would purr even louder. She was so proud of him. Her friends came to see Vince and they all agreed that he was a very handsome kitten.

**H**eidi made a special climbing post for him in the garden and she had hung some toys above it. She loved to see how Vince would climb up the post and then try to catch the little toys.

If he did catch them he would hang on for as long as he could and then drop down onto the grass only to run up the post again. Heidi loved the games that she played with Vince.

And so little Vince was beginning on his journey through life as Heidi's very own kitten.

What was ahead of him?

# LET'S FIND OUT!

The Adventures of Vince The Cat – Vince Goes to Paris

The Adventures of Vince The Cat – Vince Goes to Paris

As Vince grew bigger the two of them were inseparable. Vince would follow Heidi the short distance to her new school and then would be there again when she came out.

They were never apart. If they met a dog along the way, one that might bark at Vince, he would hop up into Heidi's arms or onto a wall until the dog went away. Vince was a very smart kitten.

At Heidi's new school they taught modern languages. As part of the curriculum the school would arrange exchange trips to different countries. Heidi was excited to learn that the first trip would be to Paris and she would be staying with a little girl her age who lived there.

Heidi could not bear to be separated from Vince so she asked her French teacher if he could come too. Fortunately Madame Walsh was a cat lover and she said, "Mais oui. Certainement!"

So that Vince could go too he had to visit the vet to have a vaccination to protect him against diseases. He was not very pleased about that but he was happy he would be able to go with his beloved Heidi.

Next they had to go to the passport office to have their photos taken to create their passport in order to travel to France. Heidi was so excited, and although Vince did not really know what to expect, you could tell he was excited too.

PHOTO BOOTH

The Adventures of Vince The Cat – Vince Goes to Paris

The Adventures of V____ ____ Goes to Paris

When the big day finally came Heidi left home with Vince in his carrier basket and she had their passports ready. With the rest of the school party they boarded the Eurostar, a train that travels to France through a tunnel that goes deep under the English Channel. The train travels very, very fast at 160kmh (99mph).

They looked out of the speeding train's window as they emerged into the sunshine in France, Heidi took Vince out of his carrier and hugged him tight. This was soooo exciting!

Bonjour!

**V**ery soon they had arrived in Paris...

...THE CITY OF LOVE!

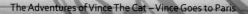

The Adventures of Vince The Cat – Vince Goes to Paris

**M**adame Walsh was in charge of the group and introduced Heidi to the little girl who's house she and Vince would be staying at during their visit.

Her name is Christelle and she has a little cat so she said, "Bonjour Heidi!, voici mon chat. Il s'appelle Tigrou." He was just the same age as Vince.

The Adventures of Vince The Cat – Vince Goes to Paris

eidi knew that Tigrou meant Tigger in English. The sweet little ginger cat had similar markings to those of the character in Winnie the Pooh. She said, "Bonjour Christelle, voici mon chat. Il s'appelle Vince."

Christelle said "Très bien! Very good! Je suis très heureuse de te rencontrer."

"I'm very pleased to meet you Christelle and I know we will have a wonderful time together in Paris," exclaimed Heidi.

Once they had settled in Christelle's 'maman' called Madame Demabre told the girls about what she had planned while Heidi was visiting.

The Adventures of Vince The Cat – Vince Goes to Paris

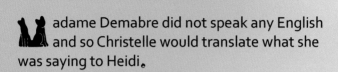 adame Demabre did not speak any English and so Christelle would translate what she was saying to Heidi.

"Nous allons visiter beaucoup de sites célèbres à Paris", said Madame Demabre. Christelle explained that this meant they were going to visit some of the most famous sites in Paris. They would be travelling by boat down the Seine, which Christelle explained was the big river that ran through Paris.

As they boarded the brightly painted boat Madame Demabre told Heidi this is called "un bateau" in French, Vince looked worried, and so did Tigrou. Heidi knew that cats usually don't like water and she whispered to Vince.

"Don't worry Vince, I'll look after you." Vince twitched his whiskers, the way he always did when he was worried and Heidi gave him a reassuring stroke.

First, they went to see the famous cathedral called Notre-Dame de Paris which Heidi learned meant Our Lady of Paris in English. She repeated the name, "Notre-Dame de Paris." It sounded very nice so she said it again. "Notre-Dame de Paris."

**C**hristelle took Heidi's hand and said, "Do you like it, mon amie?"

Mon amie meant my friend. Heidi was very pleased to be called a friend and she nodded happily.

The Adventures of Vince The Cat – Vince Goes to Paris

The next stop was at the Louvre Museum, "Musée du Louvre", in French. Heidi repeated the name in French. Musée du Louvre. Christelle's 'maman' told them that the Louvre is in the first 'arrondissement' and is the world's largest art museum and was once the palace where the king of France lived. "What is an arrondissement?" Heidi asked.

Christelle explained. "It just means a district of Paris, there are 20 arrondisements in the city."

Vince was happy, as he and Tigrou had just been watching a little mouse that was running around near where they were walking.

The museum was very big and by the time they had finished walking around it they were all quite tired. Heidi looked around as they came out of the museum door and realised she could not see Vince. Tigrou was missing too!

"Christelle, have you seen Tigrou?" Heidi called out.

"Non." Christelle said looking around.

The girls began to run around outside the museum calling the names of their cats.

"Vince! Tigrou!" they called.

Suddenly Christelle stopped and pointed up a tree.

"Ils sont là!"

And the two cats were there, having a great time, climbing up and down the tree chasing each other along branches. Their sharp claws making sure that they could climb up even the steepest tree trunk.

eow!" Heidi recognised Vince's 'come and get me' call and Tigrou obviously recognised it too, as he scampered along a branch then jumped to another with Vince following him.

It was great to see the two cats doing what they did best, climbing and running and showing just what talented acrobats they were.

Other people had spotted the two cats running up and down the trees, leaping high in the air from branch to branch and some of them were taking photos with their phones. Heidi felt very proud of her little cat.

Once they had had enough of their game the cats came back down the tree and Vince jumped up into Heidi's arms. She could feel his sides moving in and out fast as he got his breath back, and he was purring as he looked up at her. She kissed him on the head.

The Adventures of Vince The Cat – Vince Goes to Paris

Tigrou and Vince were ready for something to eat. But they would have to wait because next to see was the Eiffel Tower, "La tour Eiffel" in French.

As she had done before Heidi repeated the name of the great tower that she had been most excited to see. "La tour Eiffel," she said, "La tour Eiffel".

Christelle explained that it was named after the engineer Gustave Eiffel, whose company designed and built the tower. The tower is 324 metres (1,063 ft) tall, it has become a cultural icon of France and one of the most recognisable structures in the world.

Heidi loved it, she jumped up and down and clapped her hands while Tigrou and Vince watched the birds fluttering around the trees at the base of the tower.

𝑥𝑥 **C** 'est magnifique?  N'est-ce pas?"  Madame Demabre said.

"That means, magnificent isn't it?"  Christelle explained.  "You could answer maman by saying; Oui, c'est magnifique!  J'aime beaucoup."

"It's magnificent, I like it very much?"  Heidi guessed and Christelle smiled.

"Oui, mon amie!"

Heidi loved this new language.

It was fun to be able to talk in another language and she thought that when she was older she would make sure that she travelled all around the world and learned as many languages as possible.

Vince was loving their adventure too.  As they walked he either sat on Heidi's shoulder or walked beside her and Tigrou.  The two cats were getting on so well and getting into mischief too!  They could not resist chasing each other up the trees along the way.

eidi and Christelle liked the way that people would laugh in delight to see the cats showing off as they scampered up and down and all around the trees, sending birds tweeting up into the air.

Vince, Heidi realised was a cat who was always going to get a lot of attention, people seemed enchanted by his grey and white colouring and lots of them stopped to stroke him, even asking Heidi if they could take selfies with the little cat.

It turned out that Vince loved having his photo taken too and would pose proudly on the shoulder of anyone who wanted a photo with him.

As Heidi looked around she thought how lucky she and Vince were to be seeing the wonderful buildings and the sights and sounds of Paris together. Heidi decided she loved travelling and that she and Vince would do much more of it, would meet more new friends and learn new languages.

The adventures were just beginning and she and Vince were going to have lots more together!

They all sat down to enjoy afternoon tea and French delicacies at a Café on the Champs Elysée overlooking the Arc de Triomphe.

"The Arc de Triomphe was built to honour those who fought and died for France in the French Revolutionary and Napoleonic Wars," Christelle said.

"Oh yes I remember reading that," said Heidi, "this is a beautiful spot to see it and watch the world go by, thank you for bringing us here."

Heidi practised some of the French words she had learned with Christelle, while Vince and Tigrou were enjoying a refreshing drink of milk and watching an urban squirrel scurrying along the branch of a tree outside the café.

Christelle said, "J'ai passé une journée merveilleuse avec toi Heidi."

"I've also had a lovely day with you Christelle – Merci beaucoup. J'aime la langue Française" Heidi said. "C'est formidable!"

"I wonder where we shall visit next?"

The Adventures of Vince The Cat – Vince Goes to Paris

# FIN...
# JUSQU'À LA
# PROCHAINE
# FOIS!

The End...
until next time!

The Adventures of Vince The Cat – Vince Goes to Paris

# CATNAP
# STORIES

## FRENCH WORDS & PHRASES

In the next few pages you will find some of the French words and phrases included in this book along with some guidance on how you could pronounce some of these words.

| FRENCH | ENGLISH |
|---|---|
| Bonjour!<br>(bon-joor) | Hello!<br>Good day! or Good morning! |
| Bonsoir!<br>(bon-swar) | Good evening! |
| Salut!<br>(sah-lu) | Hi! or Bye! - this word is less formal than Bonjour! |
| voici<br>(vwa-si) | this is |
| c'est<br>(say) | this is |
| le chat<br>(le sha) | the cat |
| le chaton<br>(le sha-ton) | the kitten |
| s'appeler<br>(sapel-hay) | to be called (reflexive verb) |
| Comment tu t'appelles?<br>(Comon tu tap-el) | What's your name?<br>What are you called? |

| FRENCH | ENGLISH |
|---|---|
| Il s'appelle Vince<br>(il sap-el Vance) | His name is Vince.<br>He's called Vince |
| Très bien!<br>(tray be-an) | Very good! |
| Je suis très heureuse<br>de te rencontrer"<br>(jhe swee trays<br>heur-reuz de te<br>ron-con-tray) | I'm very pleased to<br>meet you (If you are<br>female and saying this) |
| Je serais trés heureux<br>de te rencontrer<br>(jhe se-ray trez<br>heur-ruh de te<br>ron-con-tray) | I'm very pleased to meet<br>you (If you are male and<br>saying this) |
| Maman<br>(ma-mon) | Mummy, mum |
| Ils sont là<br>(eel son la) | They are there (referring<br>to males) |
| Elles sont là<br>(el son la) | They are there (referring<br>to females) |

| FRENCH | ENGLISH |
|---|---|
| Nous allons visiter beaucoup de sites célèbres à Paris (nooz-allon vis-it-ay bow-ku de seat sell-eb-re a Pari) | We are going to visit many famous sites in Paris |
| un bateau (un ba-tow) | a boat |
| mon ami(e) (mon am-ee) | my friend (you add an 'e' after ami if your friend is female) |
| Notre-Dame de Paris (not-re dam de Pari) | Our Lady of Paris |
| Musée du Louvre (moo-zay do Loo-vre) | Louvre Museum |
| arrondisement (a-ron-deece-mont) | a district (of Paris) |
| La tour Eiffel (la tour eef-el) | the Eiffel tower |

| FRENCH | ENGLISH |
|---|---|
| C'est magnifique<br>(say man-he-fic) | It is magnificent |
| N'est-ce pas!<br>(ness-ce-pa) | Isn't it! |
| J'aime la langue<br>Française<br>(gem la laong fran-says) | I love the French language |
| C'est formidable<br>(se form-ee-da-bleur) | It's tremendous |
| J'ai passé une journée<br>merveilleuse avec toi<br>(jay pass-hay oon<br>joor-nay merv-ay-yuz<br>avek twa) | I've spent a wonderful day<br>with you |
| merci beaucoup<br>(mer-sea bo-coo) | thank you very much |
| au revoir<br>(oar -eurv-whaar) | goodbye |

This is how you conjugate the reflexive verb s'appeler in the present tense:

| | |
|---|---|
| je m'appelle | I am called |
| tu t'appelles | you are called |
| il/elle s'appelle | he/she is called |
| nous nous appelons | we are called |
| vous vous appelez | you are called (plural/ formal) |
| ils/elles s'appellent | they are called |

This is how you conjugate the verb être in the present tense:

| | |
|---|---|
| je suis | I am |
| tu es | you are |
| il/elle est | he/she is |
| nous sommes | we are |
| vous êtes | you are (plural/ formal) |
| ils/elles sont | they are |